Resilience Art

A Grief Coloring Book Using
Ritual and Music to Help You Grow

ELAINE VOCI

illustrated by
Madeline Miller

To Dana,

Peace be with
you,
Elaine

www.mascotbooks.com

Resilience Art: A Grief Coloring Book Using Ritual and Music to Help You Grow

This book is not intended as a substitute for the medical advice of physicians. The reader should regularly consult a physician in matters relating to his/her health and particularly with respect to any symptoms that may require diagnosis or medical attention.

For more information, please contact:
Mascot Books
620 Herndon Parkway #320
Herndon, VA 20170
info@mascotbooks.com

CPSIA Code: PBANG1217A
ISBN-13:978-1-68401-526-9

Printed in the United States

Resilience Art

A Grief Coloring Book Using
Ritual and Music to Help You Grow

ELAINE VOCI

illustrated by
Madeline Miller

For Greg and Todd, Jen and Helen

Table of Contents

Introduction

This coloring book is about the beauty and sorrow of grief and its relationship to resilience; it contains many personal stories and professional experiences that I share in order to illustrate aspects of grief and grieving that I have known firsthand. I hope you can use them as "nutrition" for your soul because stories are powerful and can open gateways to your inner life.

I've lived through the loss of my parents, the loss of my second husband to suicide, the loss of several special friends to old age, as well as my own experience with cancer, and a near-death experience from a serious car accident. Looking back, I can see now that each of these events opened up a place in my heart that had been unexplored and softened it, filling me with compassion for my own suffering and for the universal human suffering that is part of life. I earned a bit of wisdom each time, and I was given moments of grace that sustained me.

The grief journeys I have taken have given me the courage to keep loving others, even at the risk of one day losing them. With each loss, I become more comfortable with impermanence; I have gradually accepted that nothing lasts forever, and I know it isn't meant to. That knowing does not rob me of joy or contentment, but, rather, it deepens me, and I keep falling in love with life, again and again.

I also found that music has the power to ground me, to lighten my heavy heart, and to help me heal. The creative arts, such as drawing, writing, and photography, are wonderfully effective ways to express my sorrow and other emotions of grief. The combination of music and art encourages my natural resilience to emerge and helps me regain my emotional footing. I believe they can help you in the same way.

I want to reassure you that grief is a normal and healthy reaction to loss, and so is resilience. We all have the capacity to learn how to live with our losses and to apply our own style of grieving to the healing process. This usually takes time and happens gradually. We don't overcome grief—it's more like we make room for it in our psyche, and we find a place in which grief can co-exist with our other memories.

It is my experience that grief always brings a gift along with it. For example, grief can empower us and cause us to see the world in a different light, and, thus, it can be the spark that pushes us to say "yes" to life and make a move, change careers, get married, or leave relationships that are not healthy. Grief is a response to the loss of a loved one and a reminder that someday we will die too, and that knowledge is a gift. When we know we don't have forever, it can help us live each day with mindful awareness and remember to show our love to those who are important to us. As my father used to say, "Don't wait to give flowers until the funeral; give bouquets now while the person is alive."

Four years ago, I was trained in the art of ceremony, rites of passage, and rituals through being certified as a Life-Cycle Celebrant®. Since then, I have incorporated simple rituals into my daily life as an accompaniment to morning prayers, walking my dog, cooking, and preparing for community events that I offer, such as quarterly Death Cafes. I have also added rituals into my coaching with clients who are undergoing significant life transitions in order to help them honor and respect the meaning of these changes in their lives.

I encourage you to learn more about rituals so that you can add them to your resilience-building resources. In my private practice as a life coach, I'm creating a workshop in which I will show attendees how to use this coloring book to self-nurture and to help honor the pain of grief and transform it into healing. While my workshops are held in Indianapolis, I encourage you to explore opportunities and workshops in your own community where creative rituals are used for building resilience and dealing with grief.

How This Book Came To Be

The vision of this book appeared in my mind's eye one April morning upon awakening. I had just finished a project, a musical concert titled "Music for the Soul: Celebrating Life and Facing Death" that I sponsored and hosted in my community. It featured two hours with a wonderful folk singer, Bill Cohen, whose music made the audience and me smile, tear up a little, and feel a sweet nostalgia. The concert had taken a year to plan, organize, and promote. When it was over, I felt a great sense of joy, contentment, and relief. I thought, *Well, now I will just relax and enjoy the summer*. It turns out that Spirit had other ideas.

The concert had been held on a Sunday, and the vision for this book arrived the following Tuesday morning. Clearly, Spirit intended that this grief coloring book was ready to be born and that I was to be the midwife chosen for its labor and delivery. I have written six books, and each one has first belonged to Spirit before being given to me.

I felt a familiar feeling that always happens when divine inspiration arrives: a feeling of quickening, excitement, and rising energy in my body. I have come to recognize this as my intuition speaking to me, and I welcome its voice.

Intuition is one of my best mentors; it has guided me through many life-changing decisions and transitions. It is the finest of all mentors because it wants only the best for me and the larger world to which I belong. It knows the impact that my inspired actions will have in the grand scheme of things to serve the Greater Good. It invites me to act on the nudges that it gently gives me and celebrates my courage when I follow those nudges. It offers me unconditional love and affection, and it conveys over and over to me a simple message: "I believe in you."

It's reciprocal: I trust my intuition. I accepted the invitation to create a book, which is now in your hands. Even if the only thing you read in my book is this introduction, please take my words into your heart and embrace these truths that I have been taught by grief:

- Death ends a life, but not a relationship. Your relationship will go on as long as you can remember; it is our memories and our stories that keep that person alive in our hearts and our souls.

- Resilience is a natural ability; it does not keep us safe from the pain of grief, but coupled with self-compassion, it is the fuel that helps us figure out how to cope, adapt, adjust, and go on living.

- Sorrow doesn't last forever; one day you will wake up and not feel the same level of pain and suffering you have been feeling. Something will have shifted.

- You can't rush grief. Some people seem to believe that grief is something you can get over, like having the flu, but grief will take all the time it needs to be imprinted on your soul and gradually integrated.

- A broken heart needs to be comforted, free of your own judgment and the judgment of others, in order to heal. Your way of grieving is uniquely yours, just like your fingerprints are like no one else's. As long as your style doesn't hurt you or anyone else, it's within normal boundaries.

- Grief will change you forever; the "old" you is no longer present or retrievable. Let go of that old identity, and let yourself feel your pain fully without resistance. Listen to your inner wisdom, and you will naturally evolve into a new version of you. This version is older, wiser, and worth celebrating one day in a blessing ceremony.

Finding Our Way Home

I invite you to consider this proposal: when we are elders, approaching our last days on this earth, and we reflect on how well we did living our life to the fullest, three simple questions will focus our attention:

- Did I love well?

- Was my life meaningful?

- Did I fulfill my life's purpose?

Grief and loss have never held me back from living my answers to these questions. It is during the times of my deepest sorrows that I have devoted myself even more to these aspirations:

- Having my heart cracked open allowed me to give and receive more love.

- Writing eulogies for those I loved who died helped me see more clearly where meaning could be found.

- Wise teachers have taught me to assume that my life's mission won't end until I take my last breath, that I should keep learning and stay open to change so that I can continue to give my time and talents where they are needed.

Chapter One

What We Know About Resilience and Grieving

The good news is that for most of us, grief is not overwhelming or unending. As frightening as the pain of loss can be, most of us are resilient.

– George A. Bonnano, PhD, in *The Other Side of Sadness*

Resilience is prevalent in our culture, and resilient people widely differ in how they adapt to loss. As a society, we seem to underestimate just how resilient we are, and we don't fully understand the significant individual differences in how people grieve. One person may cry all the time when their loss is new and raw emotionally; another may not cry at all and even question themselves about whether they are "normal" in this response. (They are.) The same person can go through grief differently each time it happens, and no two experiences are exactly the same. Let me illustrate by telling you the following stories of losing my parents:

When my father died, after suffering for ten years from Parkinson's disease, I felt more relief than sorrow. The sentiment that best expressed my emotions was "Free at last. Free at last. Thank God Almighty, we are free at last," from the famous 1963 speech given by Martin Luther King, Jr. titled, "I Have a Dream." My poor Dad had suffered so many indignities, so much pain, and so much loss of independence from this dreadful disease that it broke my heart. When he died, I was deeply grateful that he was free from suffering. I mourned no longer being able to visit with him, but he had been through enough. It would have been selfish of me to want his life prolonged past the point where he no longer had a good quality of life. I grieved, and I recovered in a few months. I still had times when I felt bereft, but they became less and less frequent as the first year without him unfolded.

When my mother died fifteen years later, I felt an immediate, deep void and inconsolable sorrow for losing one of my best friends, a trusted confidante, and an amazing role model for being a kind mom and a wise and compassionate grandma. My feelings of sadness were acute and set me adrift. I felt alone, even though my sisters and family members grieved right alongside me. Sorrow came in waves and at unexpected moments; once I was in the grocery store, and a song began to play that reminded me of her, and I felt myself starting to sob. I abandoned my cart, left the store hurriedly, and got into my car crying. The pain of my loss overwhelmed me at times. During the first year after her death, the sense of loss slowly receded, and I gradually returned to my normal daily routines. It's been seventeen years as I write these words, and I still miss her.

My contrasting reactions to losing each of my parents is an example of how grief varies, not just among different people, but even within the same person. Here's what else we know about grief and resilience:

- Grief is a universal human experience but also very personal; each person grieves in their own unique way. According to Alan Wolfelt, PhD (2016) "[Grief] is neither predictable nor orderly."

- Crying is a normal part of grieving in our American culture; tears bring relief and provide a balancing mechanism that helps the body, mind, and spirit achieve equilibrium. Crying helps release emotions and should not be stifled or held back, but encouraged and accepted as a part of the healing process as the heart mends. It's always sad to me when someone who is mourning will apologize for crying as if it's inappropriate, when, in fact, it is the most understandable of reactions to a broken heart.

- The famous work of Elisabeth Kübler-Ross describes five stages that dying people go through, and they are often mistakenly applied to grieving over another person's death, which is not the same experience. There is growing agreement among death educators that grieving does not follow a set of stages.

- Many people who grieve will heal themselves and recover from their grief on their own with no need of professional help. This is evidence of a natural resilience that is hard-wired into human beings.

- No one can grieve for twenty-four hours a day; there are periods of respite from sadness that come from instances of humor, joy, laughter, and hope that make grief bearable and are like rays of sunshine to the mourner's spirit, mind, and body. It is normal to have a range of emotions when we grieve; it is not a sign of avoidance or denial of our grief if we laugh or smile. These reactions should not raise suspicions or cause harsh judgments to be made about the quality of love that the griever had for the deceased.

- The goal of grieving is not to "get over it" but to become reconciled to the significant change in our lives that has happened. Grief cannot and should not be rushed. For a small number of people, grief can become prolonged and chronic, but most of us will integrate our loss and accept what cannot be undone. This is a process, over an indeterminate time, of moving toward restored wholeness.

When we look more closely at grieving, we understand that it is about more than loss; it is also a major event in our growth as human beings that can provoke an existential questioning of what matters most to us in life. Grief forces us to look at ourselves and others through a new lens, and many times, it prompts us to make a courageous change in how we live. Sorrow can deepen us, expand our interpersonal connections with one another, and lead us to a new sense of meaning and purpose in life that is born from a dramatic change in perspective. As author Krista Tippett writes in her 2016 best-selling book, *Becoming Wise*, "To nurture a resilient human being…is to build in an expectation of adversity, a capacity for inevitable vulnerability…a way of being that can meet the range of emotions and experiences, light and dark, that add up to a life. Resilience is at once proactive, pragmatic, and humble."

What Resilient People Do to Cope with Loss

All of us have the ability to be resilient. According to Dr. Bonnano (2009), "Resilience in the face of loss is real, prevalent, and enduring." Some people are more resilient than others; genetic research may one day reveal to us the extent to which genetic factors play a role. Thanks to ongoing research into grief, we have gained a better understanding of what resilient people do to cope with the loss of a loved one:

- They talk about, and think about, their loved one often, remembering and being comforted by their memories. This was a central activity in the bereavement groups I helped facilitate. Participants frequently told stories of their loved ones to each other by sharing memories, bringing in photos, and calling to mind many positive life experiences. One woman brought in a painting of her spouse on their wedding anniversary and told us the story of how they met and some of the shared memories of their forty years together. It was a wonderful experience for all of us, and it brought us closer as a group. We would often remind one another that "death ends a life but not a relationship," and storytelling kept the memory of their loved ones alive.

- They do not rely on defense mechanisms, such as avoidance or distraction, to cope with grief; instead, they choose to engage with it directly by intentionally revisiting their memories and emotions when they are best able to tolerate the sadness. I was touched when my older sister told me that she had created a simple ritual after my mother died: she gave herself permission to "have a good cry" every night when she was soaking in the tub prior to going to bed. The warm water, the privacy of the bathroom, and using time alone to reflect on her thoughts and memories of our mom gave her a place in which to cry while fully facing her sadness. It served her well.

- They show a psychological flexibility to adapt to the challenges of their circumstances with an inner optimism, confidence, and faith in the belief that life will get better. At the funeral of Erma Bombeck, an American humorist, her friend Shirley said that "Erma's life was marked by a characteristic courage…She was so up, so enthusiastic that everything would work out." What many of her fans did not realize until after she had died was that Erma had quietly endured five years waiting for a donated kidney and died from complications soon after the transplant surgery. She often expressed hope that when she died, she would be able to answer God's questions, such as, "What have you got left of your life?" and "Any unused talent that we gave you when you were born?" by saying, "I've nothing to return. I spent everything you gave me." (DeChant 2011)

- They may engage in personal and private rituals done alone, often instinctively knowing what they need in order to comfort themselves. While public rituals (funerals, for example) help a community of people face and accept death, private rituals are not for the benefit of anyone but the mourner. One of my clients had been working with me for six months to find a new job when her husband died suddenly at home, while she, her daughter, and her parents were driving to a summer cottage where he had planned to join them.

The shock of his sudden death was overwhelming, and in the first few months that followed, she could barely manage her daily routines in order to care for herself and her teenage daughter. But one thing she did every week was to read one of the small love notes she had saved that he had written over eighteen years of marriage. He enjoyed surprising her by hiding them around the house. It was their own private romantic ritual. Reading his handwritten notes made her feel that his love was still alive and available to her, even if his physical presence was not. As she told me, "I have a corner of my heart that is, and always will be, reserved just for Mark. His love notes are a symbol of our love that is still ongoing and will be everlasting for as long as I live."

We can learn from one another, and it's important for each of us to hear our stories of love, courage, grief, and resilience. Storytelling has a profound power to heal. I have always been moved by stories of ordinary people who are truly heroes because their actions carry deep meaning, inspiration, and hope for the rest of us. Have you ever noticed that when people tell their stories to us that we discover things about ourselves? And have you ever noticed that stories about death are really stories about life? Life and death are two sides of the same coin—you can't have one without the other.

The first book I wrote was about ordinary women doing extraordinary things. They were a wonderful group of women whose stories had heart, courage, faith, and devotion to causes that were greater than themselves. That collection of stories prompted some readers to write me or email me their own stories of how they had been impacted by the women they read about. It reminded me of how a pebble tossed in a pond will cause ripples that reach the edges of the shore. We are all touched by one another's life stories, and what we say and the examples we are to others can have a lasting impact. Life is impermanent, but our stories can go on long after we are gone.

We walk on the earth knowing that the angel of Death is near us at all times and that life is impermanent, and we may take comfort in the words of a Lebanese poet, Kahlil Gibran (1923) who wisely wrote, "If you would indeed behold the spirit of death, open your heart wide unto the body of life. For life and death are one, even as the river and the sea are one."

Chapter Two

Resilience Through Art, Music, and Spiritual Experiences

Resilience is all about being able to overcome the unexpected…The goal of resilience is to thrive.

– Jamais Cascio, *The Next Big Thing: Resilience*

Loss and suffering are part of the human experience that we share with our fellow human beings. Suffering can deepen our emotional maturity and growth, or it can be a source of prolonged emotional distress and bitterness—it's largely our choice. When we choose to grow from pain and the inevitable crises of life, we are building and using our inner resilience. We sometimes speak of resilience as the ability to "bounce back" from challenges that may initially overwhelm and frighten us. I believe that it is an essential life skill—one that we will use over and over again as we mature, continuously reinvent ourselves, and decide anew, in the face of loss, that life is still worthwhile.

When I was a graduate student, I was trained as an interviewer for a major study done by the Indiana University School of Medicine and the Kinsey Institute on the effects of spinal cord injuries on human sexuality. Over an eighteen-month period, I was assigned a number of people to interview, among them two participants who deepened my understanding of human resilience. Both were men, close in age, who had sustained the same level of injury to the spinal cord while diving into fresh water lakes.

When I arrived at the first man's home in South Bend, the blinds were pulled down, and his parents somberly greeted me at the door. They showed me to a back bedroom where I found their son, a bitter young man who was angry at God for "letting this happen," and who had shunned his friends because he didn't want their "pity." He had dropped out of college and had chosen to let his world shrink to one bedroom with a TV and a few books. His answers to my questions were terse, tense, and defensive; it was a relief to finish the interview and depart that oppressive space filled with his self-pity and rage.

A few weeks later, I drove to the second man's house in Columbus and parked behind his van, which had been adapted so that he could drive using hand controls. He greeted me at the door, smiling while holding his baby daughter in his arms, and introduced me to his wife, a nurse he had wooed and won while recuperating at the Chicago Rehab Institute. They had prepared a wonderful lunch, which we eagerly enjoyed while chatting, and then he and I retired to a back porch for the interview. He told me that he viewed his injury as an "inconvenience" and that we were all "disabled" in some way. After learning to navigate the world from a wheelchair, he had returned to college and graduated, been hired by a reputable company in the community, and gotten married. In his free time, he coached a Little League team. My interview with him was a delight; he was a good storyteller, enthusiastic, and witty, and he gave sincere answers to my questions with a refreshing openness and candor. I was buoyed by his love of life and the resilience with which he had come back from such devastating injuries. I drove away feeling grateful to have met such a happy person.

I couldn't help but be struck by the difference in attitude of these two men toward their life-changing injuries, and I have never forgotten them. I learned that happiness in life is pretty much an inside job, and it isn't so much what happens to us as how we take it. As noted psychiatrist John Woodall, MD, founder of the Unity Project based in Newtown, Connecticut, observed in his 2013 article "Can We Have a 21st Century Conversation?," "Suffering expands or contracts us. Growth is not a guarantee. It is a choice."

Some of the life experiences we have in common with all of humanity are loss and suffering and the process of grieving that follows. According to Dr. Woodall (2011), who leads resilience-building programs around the world, "Grief is a measure of how much you love the person who is gone. A strong grief response is another way of saying that you love that person very much. But that love needs to evolve into a new expression, one that brings you back toward wholeness, connectivity, and unity. The work of grief is to find a new way to love. It's an act of real faith to say, 'Despite my suffering, I will remain loving.'"

I believe there are many tools and resources that can help us do that, but in this coloring book, I want to devote our search for understanding to three forms of resilience-building: art, music, and spiritual experiences done in concert with simple rites of passage, daily rituals, and ceremonies that help you engage mindfully with your personal world.

Building Resilience Through Art

When I am coloring, taking photos, or sketching, art helps me communicate my feelings without words. It helps me express my emotions, gives me insight, and raises my conscious awareness of how I am thinking, seeing, and feeling the events of my life. Empowered by that knowledge, I am free to change how I think, see, and feel about those things. In that sense, art is a positive disruptor—it can help us create a new narrative for our lives, giving us hope and inspiring us to appreciate the joy and delights around us in order to successfully transform ourselves in the ways that matter to us.

For example, at an earlier time in my life, I was going through a painful divorce and decided to take a drawing class at the local art center to get my mind off my suffering and to look forward to an activity that brought me pleasure. Surrounded by like-minded adults and a sensitive instructor, my creativity and imagination were set loose in our weekly gatherings. I began to work my way through much of the pain, sadness, and anger that I had inside. Art helped me heal, adjust to my new life, and begin to thrive again by enabling me to work on my grief from the inside out.

Drawing also helped me connect with fellow students and my instructor by gradually enabling me to tell my story and be transparent without having to use words to describe my journey. On the last day of class, the teacher invited each of us to choose our favorite drawing and explain in our own words its meaning and importance to us. That was a significant experience for me and allowed me to see my own progress, healing, and resolution. I felt supported and affirmed when the teacher asked for comments after I made my remarks, and it turned out that others in the class had also been through the special loss and pain of divorce. I felt understood and no longer alone. I grew in resilience.

Cathy Malchiodi, PhD, wrote in Psychology Today (2015) that "the resilience-enhancing capacities of art expression are not found in any one particular art-based activity, but within the characteristics of art-making itself." I agree, and while my favorites include drawing, photography, and coloring, there are other forms of art-based activities that offer the same therapeutic benefits, such as writing poetry, storytelling, and acting.

Art adds to our quality of life, and the sense of mastery it gives us builds self-confidence and personal power. We are enriched by art with its inherent life-affirming capacity for resilience. According to the Mayo Clinic, "Resilience won't make your problems go away, but resilience can give you the ability to see past them, find enjoyment in life and better handle stress." (Mayo Clinic staff, 2017)

Building Resilience Through Music

Music and sound are among the world's earliest medicines to cure illness and help restore wholeness to those suffering from mental, emotional, or physical distress. In "Music, Medicine, Healing, and the Genome Project," from the journal *Psychiatry, MMC* of the National Institutes of Health in the US National Library of Medicine, Assad Meymandi, MD, PhD, (2009) wrote that "Greek physicians used flutes, lyres, and zitters to heal their patients. They used vibration to aid in digestion, treat mental disturbance, and induce sleep…. Ancient Egyptians described musical incantations for healing the sick."

Chanting, meditative music, and nature's sounds are a few of the musical forms that serve to uplift, energize, and restore us, keeping us healthy and balanced. Music requires no translation or words; it is a universal language.

In 2016, the Harvard Health Publication, "How Music Can Help You Heal," described benefits of music therapy in which "Those who listened to music before their procedure had less anxiety and less need for sedatives. People who listened to music in the operating room reported less discomfort during their procedure. And those who heard music in the recovery room used less opioid medication for pain." (Harvard Women's Health Watch, 2016)

Listening to music is an effective treatment for mental health issues. I know from professional experience—counseling clients in alcohol and drug abuse treatment programs—that music and meditation are a potent combination that help build resilience by reducing physical pain, producing an increased sense of calmness, and lowering the thresholds of emotional distress.

Music can add to the quality of life for those with Alzheimer's by helping them manage their emotions, focus their attention, increase awareness, and adapt to their environment. Popular songs from the forties and fifties, semi-classical, Latin rhythms, and New Age music are all soothing to those suffering with Alzheimer's or dementia. The resilient effects seem to last for several hours afterward and include improved mood, increased socialization, better appetite, and reduced agitation. These may sound like small and temporary improvements, but to someone suffering daily assaults on memory, cognition, and awareness, they are blessed respites and sources of gratitude and appreciation.

When we face a serious illness, or when it happens to someone we love, music can bring a great deal of comfort and be a soothing companion. It can help acknowledge painful feelings, distract from depressing thoughts, and console us, giving us the strength to go on. Music doesn't abandon us during our times of greatest need for emotional and spiritual comfort.

The night my mother died, I drove home from the hospital under a sky that was a blanket of deep blue with bright shining stars overhead. As I looked up at them, I wondered if she was in the heavens and pondered what a full life she had led. My heart was heavy, and I felt the full force of the inconsolable loss I was facing; at the same time, I felt grateful that she had left her weary body behind and was no longer suffering physical distress.

About two weeks after her funeral, I was given a tape of music with beautiful lyrics and songs from a good friend. This collection of music, so lovingly organized, helped me in my grieving process and felt very special to me, both comforting and reassuring. I didn't feel so alone in my grief, and I had music to remind me that there is order and sense to be found in life, death, and grieving. Many times during that first year of bereavement, I turned to that tape to be uplifted and inspired by the memories of my mom that the music elicited in me. I know that my resilience grew each time I listened.

I graduated as a Life-Cycle Celebrant® four years ago at the Celebrant Institute & Foundation (www.celebrantinstitute.org/become-a-celebrant. html) and joined a profession in which officiants are trained in the art of ceremony, rituals, and rites of passage. We design and deliver personalized ceremonies that serve the needs of society and individuals to mark the important transitions in life. In my studies, I was taught that music plays a central role in diverse rites of passage, rituals, and celebrations. It is a part of every religion; sacred music takes many forms, such as chants, hymns, and prayers set to music. My personal favorites are harp and cello music—their sounds are hauntingly beautiful and bring us deeper into prayer, quiet reflection, and peacefulness, perfect for a funeral, the bedside of someone dying, or at any time when we want to feel close to creation and to the universe.

I have officiated at weddings, funerals, new home blessings, "moving away" farewell teas, and retirement celebrations, for example, and in each of them, music chosen by the clients played an important role in contributing to the meaningfulness of the event.

Building Resilience Through Spiritual Experiences

I believe that we are hard-wired for coping with loss and that some of our coping requires simple, ordinary settings that help us find a path to healing. Among the most powerful are the natural settings in our world, such as parks, large bodies of water, green spaces, public fields of grass, trees, and flowers, inhabited by birds and other living creatures with whom we share this earth. The experiences of beauty found in these settings strengthen us and offer us the chance to calm ourselves.

When I counseled alcoholics and drug abusers in treatment, one of the best and most frequent prescriptions given to clients by their psychiatrists was to go for a walk on the grounds, find a bench under a tree on which to sit, and to journal their thoughts and feelings. Even if the skies were not always blue, and the sun wasn't always shining, the air, trees, and energy from the earth had the power to transform the ordinary into the sacred. Clients, even those who claimed no religious beliefs, would often speak of finding "God" or a "Higher Power" in nature, a tree, or flowers.

There are many kinds of spiritual experiences that can bring resilience. Some are known as "noetic" experiences, events that foster inner wisdom through direct knowing and a subjective understanding that is deeply personal. I have had a number of these in my own life, and one occurred a few months after my father died. I was riding in a car with my mom as she drove to visit my Aunt "Dutchie," my father's only sister who was a gracious host and a wonderful cook. They had been close. I suddenly had a strong sense that my father was with us; I felt that he was joining us and was very happy that we were going to see her. Instead of feeling afraid or uncomfortable, I felt at ease and happy that my dad was close to us again, not in the physical world, but in the spiritual realm.

When we got to my aunt's house, she greeted us warmly at the door and said, "I'm so glad to see you...your Dad has been on my mind so strongly all morning, and I was remembering how he loved my butter cookies as I put them out on the tray a little bit ago. It's almost like he's been here with me getting ready for our visit." When I told her of my experience, we all smiled at each other and then shared a comforting afternoon together, telling stories and remembering my father's foibles, big heart, and strong will.

I heard similar stories from widows and widowers in the bereavement groups I facilitated for three years; whenever someone would share a story about feeling the presence of a loved one who had died, I noticed how the room always got quiet, and how people listened with rapt attention to the storyteller. Typically, one person's story would prompt others to share theirs. The energy in the room would brighten, and all tension would slip away, replaced with a mix of relaxed and quiet interest. Sometimes there were tears as speakers related their unusual happenings, but they were tears of joy, and there was laughter, too, at the delight they felt in being able to talk about these things with like-minded others who affirmed the mystery of life and death.

Such sharing is resilience-building and can bring a room full of strangers into a close bond that strengthens the entire group. This is a powerful benefit of peer support groups. In these healing circumstances, I think that two things are happening at once: storytellers are building resilience by sharing their memories, which helps to relieve some of the sadness and loss they feel, while listeners are gaining resilience as they absorb the stories and are comforted by the implications for themselves and their own grief journeys.

Whatever your definition of spiritual experiences, they can be profoundly liberating and can give us the opportunity to understand more of life when we approach them with an open mind and a reverence for the sacred. Spirituality reflects the wisdom we have gained, and the life experiences and teachers we have encountered, that shapes our world-view of death and dying, as well as our understanding of how to live with meaning and purpose. The resulting inner strengths, among them our emotional resilience, enable us to face and deal with many kinds of losses while deepening our appreciation for how precious life is.

Chapter Three

The Power of Rituals

Give sorrow words. The grief that does not speak whispers the o'erfraught heart and bids it break.

– William Shakespeare, *MacBeth*

Rituals are everywhere; they are ageless, timeless, global, and transformative. Rituals are not just for the big, formal, and public things in life—they are also a powerful tool for private, small, and personal events. Every ritual has an intended audience, even if it's just ourselves. We are inherently "actors on the stage of life," and rituals are performances filled with symbolism in which ordinary objects become sacred, and the stories we tell are part of a larger narrative about the meaning and purpose of our lives.

In an earlier time, traditional rituals gave people a way to process and channel feelings, values, and life experiences that were both positive, such as the birth of a child, and those that were difficult, such as a death in the family. For example, a hundred years ago when someone died, the family put a black wreath on the front door of their home to communicate that event to others. Mourners wore black armbands for a length of time to symbolize their loss, to alert others to their changed social status, and to help them transition through the bereavement process. The deceased was waked at home, the body washed, prepared, and dressed by the family and then placed in a wooden coffin in the living room, where friends, family, and neighbors gathered to mourn and give support to family members. These ritualized actions gave meaning and dignity to death, and provided a set of structured "rules" that people could follow to make their safe passage through a sorrowful, fearful, and difficult human experience. Over time, these rituals instilled a sense of connectedness and built healthy bonds that strengthened the whole community.

Contemporary rituals, especially those that help people transition from life to death, help heal the pain of saying goodbye for those who survive while also helping the dying person have a "good" and peaceful death. End-of-life rituals can be understood to include attention paid to the colors, scents, and cleanliness that create sacred space around the dying person, along with intentionally chosen poetry, prayer, and music of significance to the dying person and their family. Music is magical because it doesn't require us to think about it as we listen, and even if it's played softly in the background, it supports us by communicating directly with the soul in a primal and spiritual language of meaning.

Rituals have the power to transform the ordinary into the sacred. For example, when I prepare a meeting room for a Death Cafe, my goal is to create a space in which participants will feel safe and comfortable and that will honor our conversation. I bring fresh flowers and a mandala tablecloth I have had for many years, upon which I place items such as glass angel figurines, votive candles, colored glass hearts, a "Love" statue, and a crystal pyramid. These items represent hope, love, and spirituality; they invite reflection and inspiration. I play soft and uplifting music on a CD as people enter the room, and when I am ready to begin the meeting, I shut it off and gently strike a Tibetan singing bowl with a small wooden mallet to center us in the timeless echoes it produces. These ritualized actions help me prepare to receive people, to bless the space we occupy, and to bring a clear and focused attention to the conversations that will arise.

When combined with art, music, and other forms of artistic expression, rituals can help us undergo significant transformations and transitions in life, and, in the process, build emotional resilience that fosters understanding of the mystery of life and helps us gain a sense of mastery of how to live fully.

Managing transitions in life can be quite challenging; rituals perform an important service by acknowledging the outward manifestations of an inner change. They make the transition tangible and psychologically real to us and to those around us. Without ritual, rites of passage, and ceremonies, we are apt to feel uncertain about how to proceed, and we may get "stuck" in the past, unable to move ahead into the future and embrace the changes underway.

In my training as a Life-Cycle Celebrant®, my class was introduced to the writing of Arnold van Gennep, author of *The Rites of Passage* (The University of Chicago Press, 1960), who identified three interrelated processes that we go through over and over again in our lives, and he termed them "separation, transition, and incorporation."

- **Separation** occurs when we leave an old identity behind. For example, my eleven-year-old grandchild Kate just went through a "graduation ceremony" from elementary school. It made it clear to her that she is leaving a place and time in her life to which she will never return. The past was fondly remembered, and all that she had studied and learned was celebrated.

- **Transition** is that in-between time when we are no longer in the past but not yet fully in the future. For Kate, that will be the coming summer months when she will be preparing to enter middle school. She may look back often at elementary school and spend an equal time daydreaming about what middle school will be like.

- **Incorporation** happens when we integrate a new status in our lives. In the fall, Kate will join a sixth grade class and learn her way around a new building with new rules, teachers, and classmates. Over a few weeks' time, she will integrate her new status as a sixth-grader into her daily routines until it is a familiar school experience. Thanks, in large part, to that graduation ritual, she will successfully pass from elementary to middle school.

Rituals often relate to the archetypes of death and rebirth, which are subconsciously rooted in our human psyche. There is a universal feeling in human beings that we *must* grow, change, mature, make progress, and advance in life. Just as nature goes through endless cycles during the year known as "seasons," so do human beings experience ongoing cycles of growth and renewal. Rituals help recognize these continual rebirth

22

experiences by helping us enact the "hero's journey" with symbolism and celebrate the turning points, milestones, and other landmarks of our personal life journeys. Just as street signs help orient us to our physical location, rituals create markers that help orient us to our current stage of life, adding color and texture to our personal narratives.

To deal with the experiences of grief and loss in my life, I have found that expressing my feelings through rituals and creative arts has helped me find a path to healing. Grief takes us to places where words alone are inadequate. But visual images, rituals with music, and various forms of art, such as coloring, painting, and photography, have all helped me transcend the limitations of language and reach my deepest emotions in order to express them. In the hospice where I was a volunteer for three years, the walls were adorned with paintings done in watercolor, oil, and pastels that were created by dying patients. They were hung in hallways walked by current patients and their families and gave silent homage to those who had preceded them.

You may not see yourself as creative, but using rituals during grief isn't about becoming a skilled artist or a genius at creating ceremonies; it's about expressing your feelings in order to heal sorrow. Rituals provide meaningful ways to express grief, to help you keep your emotional footing while mourning, to reduce the inner turbulence of loss and sorrow, and to help you feel more in control. As you engage mindfully in simple ritualized actions, such as lighting a candle, listening to music, and reciting a prayer, you are purposefully and gradually integrating loss into your life story and orienting yourself to a new identity.

Rituals encourage a connection with our physical world and with our physical selves, and they literally slow us down. When we do the ordinary things in life with conscious intention and awareness, we are alive to the present moment, in the now, and we find it settles us down and reorients us to where our bodies are in time and space. Freed from our emotional pain and concerns, we are restored and nourished. Having a respite from the tumultuous disruption of loss, that calls everything into question, is life-giving and reassuring.

For example, when I sketch or create something written, I often lose all track of time as I get into a "flow state" of intense, yet effortless, concentration. In some spiritual practices, monks and nuns ritualize many of their daily activities so that they can free their minds to move to a higher level or spiritual plane. They may pray the rosary while sitting still, or kneeling, or sitting in zazen while continuously reciting a one-word chant, which brings immediate feelings of reverence and humility and, over time, builds "muscle memory" through repetition.

This grief coloring book contains a collection of coloring pages that you can combine with simple rituals to build inner resilience and support your journey through grief. To illustrate, here are six simple examples:

- Borrow a custom from Japan: purposely create a family shrine or small altar in a bedroom of your home to honor your loved one with a favorite photo, a candle, some fresh flowers, and incense. This can be a place where you begin your day with brief meditations and prayers for that person and where you can return during the day, or in the evening, for a chat before you go to sleep. Keep the shrine fresh and clean; with each act of care that you render, do it mindfully and intentionally.

- Begin to take photos that express how you feel each day or each week; date them and notice how your feelings evolve over time as you grieve. You might do this for the first six months following the death of your loved one. Set aside time to create a simple ritual of looking at this collection of images at a time and place of your choosing; do it alone, or invite a friend to join you, or perhaps even host a tea at your home where you can invite a group of close friends to share the experience of viewing and talking about the collection and what it has meant to you.

- Compose a series of weekly poems that reflect the nature of your relationship with family, friends, and/or your faith community as you are now living through the grieving process. Write them in a special journal, add the date to each, and if you like to sketch or color, put special touches on each page to amplify what you have written and to adorn each unique poem. Plan to look back in a year and read them over again to inform you of the growth this chapter of your life has brought you. Share it with someone or keep it private, as you prefer.

- Using water colors, oils, crayons, or ink, draw what you think you need most in your life right now. Add any words or phrases that come to you, draw to music that you have chosen that suits your mood, sprinkle your finished drawing with a favorite scent that you associate with your loved one, such as her signature cologne; frame it, or not. Do it once, or do it more often. Share it with someone, or not.

- Compose a drawing or take a photograph of what you hope your life will be like once the darkest days of your grief have subsided. Give it a title, and let it be an image that sustains you on those future days when you feel like you can't get out of bed and face the world. Consider framing it to make it into a keepsake of hope for better days to come. Put it where you can see it daily and reflect on it, noticing what may shift in your feelings as time goes on.

- Take a mindful walk in nature in a favorite place, or in an unfamiliar one, and bring a journal with you or a sketch book and drawing tools. Notice the environment as you keep an open heart and mind. Feel nature around you in its current state and sense the intention of life for you. What do the trees, the air, the sky, the flowers, and the birds intend for you right now? What gifts do you discover in the warm sunlight and in the cooler shadows?

- Find a quiet spot to sit and be silent; breathe in the air deeply. Feel the comforting and reassuring oneness of this earthly place and let yourself be fully present. Then, using your journal, or sketch-book, begin writing and/or creating images that express the feelings and insights you have until you feel done. As you arise to depart, bless the space and all living creatures in it; thank the space for being your companion. Return to your world with a new appreciation for the oneness of all life on earth, and let yourself rest in that knowing.

Mourning and grief are among the hardest things we have to endure. My hope is that this coloring book will help ease your fears and sadness and offer you an opportunity to give yourself the greatest gift of charity you can. To love yourself, to act as your own best friend while you are grieving, to connect with your soul through art, and to use music and simple rituals are acts of mercy. As the wise Buddha spoke, "You, yourself, as much as anybody in the entire universe, deserve your love and affection."

Chapter Four

Understanding Anticipatory Grief

Being deeply loved by someone gives you strength; loving someone deeply gives you courage.

– Lao Tzu

I was in the patient's chair in an exam room belonging to an ear, nose, and throat doctor to whom I had been referred, after a "CAT Scan" a week earlier had shown a small, but detectable, nodule on the left side of my throat. The doctor was palpating that area and gently asked me, "Can you feel this lump?" He guided the fingers of my right hand to that spot, and I did, indeed, feel it. He described what he thought it might be, ranging from a benign growth to a tumor, and he ordered a "fine needle biopsy" be performed to confirm a diagnosis.

27

I remember feeling as if I were in a movie, playing the part of a woman about to find out that something was seriously wrong with her body. It felt unreal, but by the time I was lying on an exam table, a week later, to have the biopsy, I had already begun to accept what was happening to me. It is my nature to be responsive to life's challenges, not to ignore, run away from, or deny them, but to figure out what my options are. When the oncologist told me that she would examine the tissue right then in a lab within the hospital and soon return to tell me the diagnosis, I felt tension rising in my body and my heart beating faster, but I was ready for it.

The door opened twenty minutes later, and before the oncologist could speak, I looked in her sad eyes and saw the diagnosis. I knew she felt badly having to tell me that I had cancer, but doctors are trained to deliver such news as calmly as they can and to present as positive a perspective as possible. She did a fine job of explaining her findings, and it was a relief to know what I was facing. I left the hospital and walked across the parking lot under a sunny April morning sky which seemed to uplift my spirits. I got into my car, called my boss, and told her that I had just learned I had papillary cell carcinoma—thyroid cancer. I told her I needed some time for myself, and I would be at work a few hours later.

This was not the life I had planned. Facing cancer—even saying the word out loud—was never something I had imagined myself doing. There's a lot of coronary illness in my family of origin, but little cancer. But here it was inside me, growing at the nape of my neck in the powerful thyroid gland, an organ that is shaped like a butterfly with its wings spread open across both sides of my windpipe in the front of my throat.

Like most people, I was unprepared for cancer. When I came to this unexpected turn in the road, I gathered my inner resilience to face the challenge: I studied it and learned everything I could about thyroid cancer, including current treatments, prognoses, the role of diet and heredity, and life expectancy. Armed with this information, I felt better able to talk about it with my two sons and close friends, as well as a few select people at work. I decided that while cancer was a formidable foe, it didn't always win, and I was going to do everything I could to overcome this health crisis and live a good life in spite of it. Obviously, those strategies paid off for me because here I am writing about it. But living with cancer—not knowing if it would take my life—that's the story that brings me to the topic of anticipatory grief.

Anticipatory grief is a term used to describe the grief process that a person undergoes before a loss actually occurs. Whether we are the patient ourselves or we are the family of the patient facing a life-threatening illness, anticipatory grief often starts when the initial diagnosis is made and when we sense that life, as we have known it, is now in jeopardy and that our tomorrows may be shorter than we had planned. Including the three years of treatment that followed my surgery, I lived in a state of anticipatory grief until I reached the milestone of having been cancer-free for five years.

Anticipatory grief has the same emotions of regular grief, including anger, sadness, and feeling alone, but these are compounded by:

- The added strain of going through difficult and often repeated treatments, such as chemotherapy and radiation, or watching a loved one go through them.

- The physical and mental exhaustion due to the daily demands of being dependent, or of being the caregiver and experiencing anger, impatience, being on edge all the time, and feeling tired.

- Emotional exhaustion that stems from a continual state of anxiety that lies just below the surface of each day—the feeling of life being out of control and the persistent uncertainty and fear of what may happen next.

With an extended illness, we grieve many losses that we fear may become permanent: the loss of stability and security, the loss of independence, the loss of future dreams and hopes that we hold dear, and the loss of a life we had planned.

Just as there are many ways to grieve, and no two grief experiences are the same, there is evidence (Reynolds and Botha 2006) that anticipatory grief can impact the intensity and duration of the overall grieving experience in one of two ways:

- For some people, it can act as a "dress rehearsal" for the day when death actually arrives, thus reducing the intensity and shortening the duration of grief when the loss finally occurs.

- For others, it can have little to no effect on the intensity and duration of grief that follows a death; the grief can be just as intense and painful as if there had been no preparation.

Either way, both are considered normal reactions. That may seem unusual, but it makes sense when we consider the different ways that people respond to stress and when we factor in other variables, such as relationship dynamics, communication between the patient and the family, past history of how the family relates to each other, and family and personal values.

There's also something else that influences anticipatory grief, and that is how society views long-term illnesses that bring about a gradual decline and, finally, death. If someone dies suddenly, in a car accident for example, or if a person dies of old age, the people around the family will provide them with support, comfort, and sympathy by sending cards, food, and by attending the funeral or memorial service. These are accepted roles and actions in our society that people are familiar with and are comfortable observing.

But there is a lack of both words and rituals that are associated with a diagnosis, for example, of cancer, dementia, or Alzheimer's disease. People may not know how important it is to offer their support and to acknowledge the grief that comes with such significant life transitions. They may avoid conversations that are uncomfortable, or they may not know what to say. These reactions further isolate the patient and their family members, and they compound the grief they are going through.

We can change that, and it's not complicated if we respond with love and compassion. If you are the one going through anticipatory grief, you may be able to help yourself if you let close friends know how you are feeling and the kind of support and help that would comfort you. Don't "should" on yourself by telling yourself that you "should be strong" or "should be able to handle the stress" and then refuse any help that is offered. This is not a time to go it alone; you need other people to get you through this journey. Give yourself the same love and compassion you would give to your best friend in these circumstances.

Let me tell you a short and true story…

When my dear friend was diagnosed with breast cancer three years ago, I understood the emotions she was feeling and the way her life had changed with that unexpected diagnosis. I decided that I would be a "chemo buddy" with her as she underwent surgery and treatment so that she would have my steady support and encouragement. I talked with her over coffee a few weeks after she had been diagnosed and told her I wanted to walk this path with her so that she would not feel isolated. I had in mind cooking meals occasionally, talking by email regularly, and just generally staying close by.

She was appreciative and pleased to accept my offer; she also told me she was glad that we could talk openly about cancer, since I was a survivor myself as well as a close friend who loved her. It was a "relief," she said, to know that I was able to tolerate such conversations.

A few days later, I was in the greeting card section of my local drugstore, and it came to me that I would like to send her a card once a week to tell her I was thinking of her. Without telling her I was going to do it, I began. For the next fifteen months, I sent her a weekly card; some were corny and humorous, some were serious and inspiring, and others were blank cards where I wrote my own verses or shared a quote or a poem that seemed to fit.

She came through all the challenges she faced with a positive attitude and wisely used meditation, music therapy, and prayer groups from within her circle of support to guide her recovery. We celebrated over lunch one sunny afternoon, and she handed me a small card on which she had handwritten the words of Maya Angelou (quoted in Gallo, 2014), "People will forget what you said, people will forget what you did, but people will never forget how you made them feel." We both cried and hugged each other in celebration of our friendship, as well as her successful passage through cancer, like two marathon runners who had completed a hard race together. It felt great!

I keep that card in a special box of mementos that hold meaning for me. Please feel free to borrow my card idea, should you have a need for it one day. Grief, in any form, is hard to bear and tests our spirit, as well as our mind and body, but nothing matches the healing power of a whole and loving heart. "Love bears all things, believes all things, hopes all things, endures all things." (1 Cor., 13:7. Revised Standard Version)

Poetry and Blessings About Death, Grief, and Resilience

The Song

By Liza Hyatt, in her collection titled, *The Mother Poems*. Reprinted by permission and published by Chatterhouse Press, Indianapolis, IN.

On the floor, weeping again,
up from the belly,
each breath sounding the depth.
Old ground gone.
Old sound.
Deeper.

My mother – almost eighty, health fading.
My daughter – fifteen, strong wings, rarely home.

The two females I've loved
with my body –
life depending on it –
are leaving me.

When my wild heart calms
I go to the woods.
To the ridge over the creek,
the new hepatica – ephemeral flowers –
love them now before they are gone –
and robins, dusk, spring frogs,
their slow rattling ahhs breathed from a hidden place.

These losses must be.
There is a voice as old as bird, as old as frog song in me
with its own rhythm, season, wisdom.
Earth gave it to people to sing. We call it grief.
And I've been singing it like I was born to.
This evening, again, I've been singing it.

Lying Awake in Fire

By Liza Hyatt, in her collection titled, *The Mother Poems*. Reprinted by permission and published by Chatterhouse Press, Indianapolis, IN.

I lie in the dark, unable to sleep,
after two days
of touching and being touched
by the things she made
(in her last week of life,
and when she was a young mother,
and when she first moved here
in her fifties, starting again
the writer's life she dreamed of in college).

I am disturbed by how fast
the last, most creative decades of her life went
and by how my own remaining allotment of time
is suddenly too short
to contain everything I need to do.

And I am awakened and alarmed by
her individual fire,
restless, impatient, pulsing.

I have been holding this fire in my hands all day
with an intimacy not known
since I was a child living in her house
when I grew in it, unconscious of it.

Her spirit, her energy,
prolific, fierce, incandescent,
surrounds me now in the dark night,
alerting, enlivening me,
pushing me toward life,
flaring and burning,
above and below and beside me.

As if some goddess is holding me in the flames,
not to spare me from death,
but to make me forever mortal.

As if I am in her again.
And from her spirit body
I am being further born.

In the First Months After Her Death

By Liza Hyatt, in her collection titled, *The Mother Poems*. Reprinted by
permission and published by Chatterhouse Press, Indianapolis, IN.

I hope for a dream of her
to reassure me she is alright.
But, not sleeping well
I don't remember my dreams.

One night, while lying awake,
I think of the animals she loved
and wonder if,
as she emerged through the tunnel into the light,
her horse Pilot
was among the souls
gathered there to greet her.
And suddenly, I see the image
of her riding bareback
through the pastures of another world,
her body ageless and full of joy,
gleefully galloping away.

One day, a memory comes
of a little pleasure she shared
with me when I visited her last June.
I sat next to her cramped and messy desk
amid piles of paper and coffee cups
and she showed me
her favorite YouTube video

of baby ducks who hatched
on the roof of a bank
(where their imperfect mother had nested)
and a man standing below
gently catching them like feathered baseballs
as they waddled over the threshold,
flightlessly falling.
"I watch this every day," she told me.
"It reminds me of the good in the world."
And this memory comforts me,
reminds me of what was tender in her.

My sleep begins to lengthen.
In dreams I know she is dead but do not see her.

Finally, I dream that,
instead of Charon and his boat over the river Styx,
she is riding in a crowded streetcar in a place like San Francisco.
She is sitting near the open door,
and there are no more seats left.
The streetcar pauses near where I am standing
and she looks right at me,
makes eye contact,
and points her finger at my face emphatically
the way she always did,
fiercely saying, "You tell him...!"
and says more that I don't remember
and then the street car pulls away
and she is talking happily with the others
kicking her feet up in the air
agile and alive in her body
excited about where they are going.

Following

By Liza Hyatt, in her collection titled, *The Mother Poems*. Reprinted by permission and published by Chatterhouse Press, Indianapolis, IN.

And even when I am in my 70's
and my hip hurts, and my own daughter,
after 4 decades of growing,
is finally choosing her Self
while having to care for and let go of me
(in whatever ways our lives, our personalities allow)
even then, my mother will be in me,
living and changing,
stubbornly undying.

She has always been ahead of me,
on the way to the pear tree, in the mall,
as woman leading child,
as woman entering midlife,
as woman growing old,
onward, onward, marching as to war
through her life, through our lives.

I will let her go, independent and alone,
when this life fades from her
and she boards the boat with white sails
to voyage beyond where I can see,
beyond where I can imagine.

But she will visit,
in memories, dreams, thoughts,
planted in my body, like seeds that will wake
only when I come to
the twists in life's road she traveled before me,
only as I reach the age she was
when she came to these choices, these crossroads.

And I will go deep down into her story bravely singing,
I will wrestle with what was monster and what was milk in her.

36

Fears will surface as I walk
from the middle of the world toward my future.
And sometimes there will come from her,
a gift, a taste of something golden, ripe, living, unexpected,
and I will follow her,
follow her,
follow her,
this woman who has been galloping, marching,
loosing and finding her way,
hurrying impatiently, limping with her cane,
pushing angrily against her walker
toward this place where we begin,
this tree of life,
this Great Mother,
this living universe
of fruitful darkness
and delicious light,
here at birth, in life,
and on the other side of death.

Do Not Stand at My Grave and Weep

Do not stand at my grave
and weep.
I am not there.
I do not sleep. I am a thousand winds
that blow.
I am the diamond glints
on snow.
I am the sunlight
on ripened grain.
I am the gentle
autumn rain.

When you awaken
In the morning's hush,
I am the swift uplifting rush
of quiet birds
in circled flight.
I am the soft stars
that shine at night.
Do not stand at my grave
and cry.
I am not there. I did not die.

– Mary Elizabeth Fyre

Crossing The Rainbow Bridge

Just this side of heaven is a place called the Rainbow Bridge. When an animal dies that has been especially close to someone here, that pet goes to the Rainbow Bridge. There are meadows and hills for all of our special friends, so they can run and play together. There is plenty of food, water, and sunshine, and our friends are warm and comfortable. All the animals who had been ill and old are restored to health and vigor. Those who were hurt or maimed are made whole and strong again, just as we remember them in our dreams of days and times gone by.

38

The animals are happy and content, except for one small thing: they each miss someone very special to them, who had to be left behind. They all run and play together, but the day comes when one suddenly stops and looks into the distance. His bright eyes are intent. His eager body quivers. Suddenly he begins to run from the group, flying over the green grass, his legs carrying him faster and faster.

You have been spotted, and when you and your special friend finally meet, you cling together in joyous reunion, never to be parted again. The happy kisses rain upon your face; your hands again caress the beloved head, and you look once more into the trusting eyes of your pet, so long gone from your life but never absent from your heart. Then you cross the Rainbow Bridge together...

– Author Unknown

A Gaelic Blessing

Deep peace of the running wave to you;
Deep peace of the flowing air to you;
Deep peace of the quiet earth to you;
Deep peace of the shining stars to you;
Deep peace of the gentle night to you;
Moon and stars pour out their healing light on you;
Deep peace to you, the light of the world to you,
Deep peace to you.

40

Books on Grief and Resilience

The Year of Magical Thinking by Joan Didian

The Other Side of Complicated Grief: Hope in the Midst of Despair by Rhonda O'Neill, RN

The Other Side of Sadness: What the New Science of Bereavement Tells Us About Life After Loss by George Bonanno, PhD

If Only by Carol Geithner

Making Toast: A Family Story by Roger Rosenblatt

An Exact Replica of a Figment of My Imagination: A Memoir by Elizabeth McCracken

Saturday Night Widows: The Adventures of Six Friends Remaking Their Lives by Becky Aikman

Healing After Loss: Daily Meditations for Working Through Grief by Martha Hickman

Option B: Facing Adversity, Building Resilience and Finding Joy by Sheryl Sandberg

Books on Death and Dying

Modern Death: How Medicine Changed the End of Life by Haider Warraich, MD

Being Mortal: Medicine and What Matters in the End by Atul Gawande, MD

How We Die: Reflections on Life's Final Chapters by Sherwin Nuland, MD

Hospice Voices: Lessons for Living at the End of Life by Eric Lindner

Dying Well by Ira Byock, MD

PJs, Pearls and Fishing Poles: A Loving Story about Hospice Honoring Patients, Families and Caregivers by Penny Davis

Knocking on Heaven's Door: Your Path to a Better Way of Death by Katy Butler

Books on Ceremony and Rituals

Sacred Dying by Megory Anderson

Life Cycle Ceremonies: A Handbook for Your Whole Life by Sheri Reda and Charlotte Eulette

The Rites of Passage by Arnold Van Gennep

Deeply Into the Bone: Reinventing Rites of Passage by Ronald Grimes

From Beginning to End: The Rituals of Our Lives by Robert Fulghum

The Art of Ritual: A Guide to Creating and Performing Your Own Rituals for Growth and Change by Renee Beck and Sydney Barbara Metrick

Remembering Well: Rituals for Celebrating Life & Mourning Death by Sarah York

Websites That Bring Comfort and Information to Those Who Grieve

www.aftertalk.com
On this site are numerous online aids to help you go through the grieving process. There are grief blogs, inspirational quotes, and interactive writing tools to help you manage your grief. One feature is written by Robert Neimeyer, PhD (Professor in the Department of Psychology, University of Memphis, and author of thirty books), and he also has radio podcasts on the site.

complicatedgrief.columbia.edu/resources/resources-public/websites/
The Center for Complicated Grief conducts clinical research that helps people with complicated grief reclaim their lives. Their innovative research and public educational efforts raise awareness of complicated grief, reducing societal stigma, and other misconceptions, and they train professionals.

www.modernloss.com
A website where people post their experiences of grief, with how-to and advice columns that explore the topics of grief and loss experiences.

thedinnerparty.org/about/
A community of mostly twenty- and thirty-somethings who have each experienced significant loss and get together over potluck dinners to talk about the ways in which it continues to affect our lives and how to thrive in a life after loss.

whatsyourgrief.com/about/
Started by two mental health counselors, this site promotes grief education, exploration, and expression in practical and creative ways. They provide the public with education, practical suggestions for moving forward from grief, ways to honor and remember deceased loved ones, and a supportive online community.

Gratitudes

Grief has made me appreciate my blessings. When something happens during the day that is a blessing, I offer up an immediate and sincere thank you to the Universe. At the end of each day, I acknowledge an inventory of blessings I am grateful for before I go to sleep. It has a soothing effect, and I feel myself relax in preparation for a restful night of restorative sleep.

In that same spirit of gratitude, I want to thank you, dear reader, and thank my Creator, for giving me the opportunity to share with you the stories, prayers, and insights from my own life. I thank the Source and Creator of my life for inspiring this book into being and for granting me the privilege of being its midwife. I thank you for choosing this book to help you color your way through grief with music, art, and rituals. I am grateful that you are a kindred spirit who was drawn to this book to help you move through your journey of grief. Our connection, through this book, is something I could never have brought about without Spirit's wisdom and guidance.

With a full heart, I also want to thank my publisher, Mascot Books, for their belief in me and in this book. They worked hard to help me share my work with you, and I am grateful to them for their expertise and interest in bringing this coloring book into the world and making it look just the way I envisioned it. I thank my editor, Karen Carpenter, whose patience and diligence helped make this book everything I wanted it to be. Karen is a wonderful soul, a talented photographer, and a fellow writer whose future blogs I know will be as special as she is.

I deeply thank all of the teachers—and Guardian Angels, seen and unseen—who have inspired, empowered, and encouraged me and enlightened my soul. I have been given so many blessings in this life of loving friends, trusted allies, wise teachers, and amazing companions, both two-legged and four-legged, like my dog Winky, that it fills me with wonder.

It's been said that a good marriage is the most precious possession a person can have, and by that standard, I am a wealthy woman. Any spouse of a writer has to be both patient and encouraging, and my husband, Al, has been both. He has supported me in every way possible, and I cannot say thank you enough.

I thank my grown children, my sons Greg and Todd, and my "daughters" Jen and Helen, who have loved me and spent many hours in family companionship, conversations, cooking together, and friendly card games. They may not have been aware of how valuable their support and love is to my creative life force or how they have each contributed something to my work. Now they know.

I also want to recognize my grandchildren: Connor, Troy, Charlie, Alex, and Kate. They always bless me and enrich my life with their bright, sparkling energy and enthusiasm. They make me proud, and they make me believe in the future.

It would be lonely to live in a world without blessings. Blessings are like thresholds we step over that bring healing and invoke profound transformations that introduce us to meaningfulness and belonging. When we give a blessing to others, one comes back to us in a never-ending circle of love. I am grateful for my blessings, and I pray that this book may be a blessing for you.

Citations by Chapter

What We Know About Resilience and Grieving

King, Martin Luther, Jr. 1963. "I Have A Dream." Speech, Washington, DC, August 28. The Martin Luther King, Jr. Research and Education Institute at Stanford University. https://kinginstitute.stanford.edu/king-papers/documents/i-have-dream-address-delivered-march-washington-jobs-and-freedom

Wolfelt, Alan, D. 2016. "Helping Dispel 5 Common Misconceptions About Grief." The Center for Loss and Life Transition, December 14. https://www.centerforloss.com/2016/12/helping-dispel-5-common-misconceptions-grief/

Kübler-Ross, Elisabeth. 1969. *On Death and Dying: What the Dying Have to Teach Doctors, Nurses, Clergy and Their Own Families*. New York: Scribner.

Tippett, Krista. 2016. *Becoming Wise: An Inquiry into the Mystery and Art of Living*, 252. New York: Penguin Press.

Bonanno, George, A. 2009. *The Other Side of Sadness: What the New Science of Bereavement Tells Us About Life After Loss,* 195. New York: Basic Books.

DeChant, Carol, compiled 2011. *Great American Catholic Eulogies*, 222. Chicago: ACTA Publications.

Gibran, Kahlil. 1923. *The Prophet*. New York: Alfred A. Knopf, Inc.

Resilience Through Art, Music, and Spiritual Experiences

Woodall, John. 2013. "Can We Have a 21st Century Conversation?" *John Woodall, MD, The Resilient Life* (blog), April 4. http://www.johnwoodall.net/2013/04/04/can-we-have-a-21st-century-conversation/#axzz4l2NIoiQl

Woodall, John. 2011. "Let's Heal the Hurt: The Heart Opens" *John Woodall, MD, The Resilient Life* (blog), December 16. http://www.johnwoodall.net/2011/12/16/lets-heal-the-hurt-the-heart-opens/#xzz4m5KqxbCU

Malchiodi, Cathy. 2015. "Art Is About Resilience, It Always Has Been." *Psychology Today*, August 31. https://www.psychologytoday.com/blog/arts-and-health/201508/art-is-about-resilience-it-always-has-been

Mayo Clinic. 2017. "Resilience: Build Skills to Endure Hardship," May 18. http://www.mayoclinic.org/tests-procedures/resilience-training/in-depth/resilience/art-20046311

Meymandi, Assad. 2009. "Music, Medicine, Healing, and the Genome Project." *Psychiatry MMC* 6(9): 43–45. https://www.ncbi.nlm.nih.gov/pmc/articles/PMC2766288/

Harvard Health Publications. 2016. "How Music Can Help You Heal," *Harvard Women's Health Watch*. http://www.health.harvard.edu/mind-and-mood/how-music-can-help-you-heal

The Power of Rituals

Gennep, Arnold van. 1960. *The Rites of Passage.* Chicago: The University of Chicago Press.

Understanding Anticipatory Grief

Reynolds, Linda, and Derek Botha. 2006. "Anticipatory Grief: Its Nature, Impact, and Reasons for Contradictory Findings." *Counselling, Psychotherapy, and Health* 2(2), 15-26. https://www.mentalhealthacademy.net/journal_archive/cph0613.pdf

Gallo, Carmine. 2014. "The Maya Angelou Quote That Will Radically Improve Your Business." *Forbes*, May 31. https://www.forbes.com/sites/carminegallo/2014/05/31/the-maya-angelou-quote-that-will-radically-improve-your-business/#70502a97118b

Resilience Art Experiential Workshop

As a companion to my book ***Resilience Art: A Grief Coloring Book Using Ritual and Music to Help You Grow,*** I have created an uplifting workshop where I will show attendees how to use my coloring book to self-nurture, and to help honor the pain of their grief and transform it into healing with creative rituals and music especially chosen for the event.

Music has the power to ground us, to lighten our heavy hearts, and to help us heal. **The creative arts are wonderfully effective ways to express sorrow and other emotions of grief,** and the combination of music and art encourages our natural resilience to emerge, and helps us regain our emotional footing.

- Grief is a normal and healthy reaction to loss, and so is resilience.

- We all have the capacity to learn how to live with our losses and to apply our own style of grieving to the healing process. This usually takes time and happens gradually.

- We don't overcome grief, we make room for it in our psyche and we find a place in which grief can co-exist with our other memories.

WHO SHOULD ATTEND

- Anyone grieving the loss of a loved one

- Family caregivers

- Professional caregivers

- Social workers, spiritual directors, grief counselors

- Activity directors of assisted living centers

WORKSHOP FORMAT

- The workshop is two hours in length.

- All coloring supplies are provided including crayons, coloring pencils, and liquid ink pens.

- Attendees are encouraged to wear comfortable loose clothing and to bring at least 1-3 items related to your grief, such as a photo of your loved one, a small figurine that symbolizes your loss, etc.

- Previous art experience is not necessary.

- The cost is $40 per person and includes the coloring book.

- For information, call Elaine at 317-730-5481

About the Author

Elaine Voci, PhD, is a life coach and a Life-Cycle Celebrant® who offers life and bereavement coaching to couples, families, and adults, and teaches workshops on Caregiving and Conscious Aging. She also facilitates a quarterly Death Cafe in her community. Her own grief experiences have helped her integrate a positive life philosophy that acknowledges life and death as two sides of the same coin. It is her sincere hope that this unique coloring book gives comfort and support to those who are making their way through grief and brings clarity, insights, and resilience for the journey. She can be reached by email at elaine@elainevoci.com.

Other books by Elaine Voci:

Bridge Builders: Ordinary Women Doing Extraordinary Things
(also available in e-book format)

Celebration of Light

Soul Sketches: How to Craft Meaningful and Authentic Eulogies
(e-book format)